THE BUSHCRAFT HANDBOOKS

TRAPPING & TRACKS

Illustrations by the Author

Richard H. Graves

The Bushcraft Handbooks
Trapping & Tracks

This Edition Copyright © 2013 by Palmer River Publishing

Cover, Graphics and Layout by: Palmer River Publishing

ISBN-13: 978-1484821695
ISBN-10: 1484821696

About The Author

The author of "The Bushcraft Handbooks", Richard Graves, is a member of the Irish literary family of that name. A veteran of the Great War campaigns in the Dardenelles and the Western Front, the author became passionate about the bush at an early age. As an enthusiastic bushwalker, skier and pioneer of white-water canoeing, he foresaw how a knowledge of bushcraft could save lives in the Second World War. To achieve this end, he initiated and led the Australian Jungle Rescue Detachment, assigned to the Far East American Air Force. This detachment of 60 specially selected A.I.F. soldiers successfully effected more than 300 rescue missions, most of which were in enemy-held territory in New Guinea, without failure of a mission or loss of a man.

An essential preliminary for rescue was survival, and it was for this purpose that the notes for these books were written. These notes were later revised and prepared for a School in Bushcraft which has been operating for several years and continues to provide valuable instruction to Servicemen embarking overseas on active service in Korea and Malaya.

Bushcraft

As far as is known, "The Bushcraft Handbooks" are unique. There is nothing quite like them, nor is any collection of published bushcraft knowledge as comprehensive.

The term "Bushcraft" is used because "woodcraft" commonly means either knowledge of local fauna and flora or else is associated with the blood-sports of hunting and shooting. "The Bushcraft Handbooks" include a volume on traps and snares, but these are purposely-designed to be completely ineffective for native animals which are insect enters or grazers. These traps have been included because they would only be effective in catching predatory animals such as cats and dogs which have taken to the bush, and other "pest" creatures such as feral swine or goat.

"Bushcraft" describes the activity of how to make use of natural materials found locally in any area. It includes many of the skills used by primitive man, and to these are added "white man" skills necessary for survival, such as time and direction, and the provision of modern "white man" comforts as illustrated in the volume on bush campcraft.

The practice of bushcraft develops in an individual a remarkable ability to adapt quickly to a changing environment. Because this is so, the activity is a valuable counter to the over-specialisation so prevalent in today's society, and is particularly significant in youth training and character-moulding work.

INTRODUCTION to the BUSHCRAFT HANDBOOKS

THE PRACTICE OF BUSHCRAFT shows many unexpected results. The five senses are sharpened, and consequently the joy of being alive is greater.

The individual's ability to adapt and improvise is developed to a remarkable degree. This in turn leads to increased self-confidence.

Self-confidence, and the ability to adapt to a changing environment and to overcome difficulties, is followed by a rapid improvement in the individual's daily work. This in turn leads to advancement and promotion.

Bushcraft, by developing adaptability, provides a broadening influence, a necessary counter to offset the narrowing influence of modern specialisation.

For this work of bushcraft all that is needed is a sharp cutting implement: knife, axe or machete. The last is the most useful. For the work, dead materials are most suitable. The practice of bushcraft conserves, and does not destroy, wild life.

R.H.G.
April, 1952

CONTENTS

TRAPPING & TRACKS

The signs animals leave on the ground can be more revealing than any book written by man, but unfortunately few people are able to see these signs and fewer still can read them.

To understand something of the behaviour of animals one must realise that the development of their senses is markedly different to mankind's, and therefore where we obtain information through our eyes and ears, one animal may obtain the same information through its sense of smell and another through its ability to detect temperature changes, or through vibrations.

Where man communicates with man through speech, some forms of animal life communicate through telepathy. You see this in a flock of pigeons which turn in flight as one bird.

This handbook broadly deals with some of these special characteristics explaining how knowledge of the 'sensitivity' of the creature is useful", and how the animal's tracks provide a reliable indicator to its habits.

The whole area covered in this book, if practised, leads to a remarkable development of one's powers of observation and deduction.

Tracks and Their Meaning

Simple Deduction

To be a successful trapper you must learn first to observe, and then to make the correct deduction from your observation. For example, if you see a bird move over the ground in a series of hops it would leave tracks like these.

You agree that these would be the tracks of a hopping bird?

To know that a bird hops on the ground tells you that *it is normally unaccustomed to being on the ground.* This is turn leads to the conclusion that, being unaccustomed to living on the ground, it therefore does not feed on the ground. Where else then might it feed?

Your answer would be that it may find its food either in the air or on shrubs or trees.

But you observe that most birds that look for food in trees walk along the branches if they feed on fruit or flower blossoms and that the birds which feed on insects hop from branch to branch. Your final deduction is that birds which leave hopping tracks on the ground are birds which capture their food (in the form of insects) in the air, and so you make a rule, 'hopping birds are insect eaters.'

In a general way this is true, but there are exceptions to all these general rules, and not all insect eating birds are hoppers, and not all ground hopping birds are insect eaters. (Consider your pet canary or the lovely painted finches, both of which are ground hopping, and both of which are grain or seed eaters.)

First, these are made by a bird which walks, not hops. Therefore it is accustomed to finding some, or all of its food on the ground. Being a ground feeding bird it may either—

feed on grain or fallen fruit,

feed on ground living creatures,

feed on flesh which it finds on the ground.

If it feeds on grain or fallen fruit it will not have the centre toe development that would be needed by a bird which had to scratch or dig for its food, nor would it have the rear claw development required by a flesh eater.

These, therefore, are the tracks of a ground feeding bird which, not having a digging claw, nor having talons, MUST be a grain or fruit eater.

Notice the development of the centre toe, and powerful claw. This is the mark of a ground feeding bird which scratches or digs for its food. It is a ground insect eater.

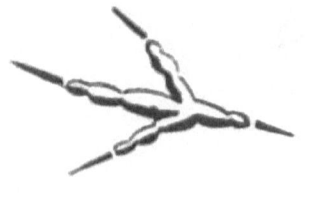

Here are four short and powerful toes with strong claws particularly on the hind toe. These are the talon feet of a ground feeder which lives on flesh. The foot tracks of a hawk and eagle, or a crow.

Naturally the place where the tracks are observed has a bearing on reading the correct answer, and if the tracks are found on the edge of a swamp or marsh the answer could be quite different from the answer if the tracks were observed a long way from water.

Tracks read as those of a grain eating ground feeder in forest land could correctly be read, if the same tracks were seen in mud, or by a reedy swamp edge, as tracks of a non-swimmimg, flesh-eating water bird.

Tracks such as these are easily and correctly read.

The web-footed track of a swimmer such as duck, swan, or geese.

Animal Tracks

In the animal kingdom the reading of tracks is equally simple. Consider these two—what is the feature you first notice?

It is the single or double thumb, the prehensile digit, which is the mark of every true tree climbing animal. Look at your own hand. Can you climb trees?

There are exceptions to this, as to the other general rules. For instance the tree climbing kangaroo of North Queensland, which has a prehensile tail. (Incidentally the domestic cat is not a true tree climber. It can 'claw' its way up a tree but. it cannot 'climb', as, say, a monkey climbs.)

In these tracks the claws of the centre toes are most prominent, and you are correct if your deduction is that these are the tracks of an earth digger, or burrower. The prehensile thumb is undeveloped, you notice.

The digging claws may be on fore or hind feet. Generally the fore feet show them most sharply, but whether on front or hind feet, they are the invariable mark of the digger.

These tracks show neither the prehensile thumb or the digging claw.

If you deduce that they are the tracks of flesh eating animals you would be correct, but why?

The answer is that the tracks show pronounced 'toes,' and that toes, when not used for climbing or digging, both of which call for special development, have another special use in that they give the foot a 'springboard' when running, and so you make the deduction that these are the tracks of fast running animals, and they are not grazing animals because no grazing animal shows 'toes,' unless you recognise the hoof of a cow or horse, sheep, etc., as 'tips' of toes or 'toenails,' which they really are.

These tracks are made by the grass and herbage eaters. Having neither climbing thumbs, to escape from enemies by climbing, nor digging tools, to escape by burrowing, their only means of escape is by running. Therefore you may decide that animals which have cloven hoofs are very fast running.

Tracks Indicate Habits

Tracks made by animals on the ground, when read correctly, show the pattern of the animal's habits. This calls for continuous and careful observation. It is important to recognise the fact that animals, and all living creatures, are as much creatures of habit as human beings. A particular animal will follow the same track to and from water day after day. It will hunt in the same area continually, and only leave the area when driven out by fire, flood or drought. Even then the move is only temporary, and it will return when conditions once again are favourable.

This 'habit-forming' characteristic of animals makes it possible for the experienced trapper to predict the animal's movements, and so he selects the sites for his traps or snares, certain that they will be visited.

In the bush you will find many animal trails. These are the 'roads' of the bush creatures. They travel over them continually backwards and forwards, to and from their resting places to their feeding grounds and favourite wateholes.

By observation of the number and newness of the tracks and droppings on these trails you can gauge the extent of animal traffic.

If you put an obstacle across one of these animal trails the animals will make a detour around the obstacle, always following the line of least resistance, and come back to the road again beyond the obstacle.

A very good example of these roads are the trails radiating from a meat ants' nest. Exactly the same pattern is repeated in jungle, forest and grassland by all animals. Examine the upward side of a leaning gum tree, and if you see scratch marks of varying ages then the tree is a 'tree road' of possums or koalas, which either live in dead hollows or come to the tree nightly to feed on the young leaves or mistletoe berries. By looking up at a tree you can quickly tell if it is a feeding tree, or a living-quarters-tree. (The latter will show many dead limbs which are hollow, and therefore comfortable living quarters for possums and phalangers.)

Animal World's 10 Senses

As human beings we experience five senses. These are: Sight, Sound, Touch, Taste, Smell. These senses are the result of very highly specialised cells. One group of these cells in our eyes are stimulated by light and colour. As a result we 'see.' So it is with all our other senses. As human beings our eyes tell us more than any of our other senses, and all senses are directed to one end . . . LIVING. By living is meant, first the finding of food which it is safe for us to eat, and then keeping ourselves out of danger, and so keeping our race or species perpetuated.

In these end purposes of the senses the whole animal and vegetable kingdom differs in no way from us. It appears to this writer that some forms of life have developed senses which are quite beyond our human experience, and therefore rather difficult for us to understand.

The full list of these senses (sensitivities) might be as follows:

Light sensitivity ⎤
Sound sensitivity ⎟
Taste sensitivity ⎬ experienced by humans
Touch sensitivity ⎟
Scent sensitivity ⎦
Temperature sensitivity
Vibration sensitivity
Supersonic sensitivity
Telepathic sensitivity
Directional sensitivity.

Note: These are purely the author's observations, and not backed by scientific proof; consequently readers are advised not to accept these or the following remarks without reservation.

These sensitivities vary in their development between one creature and another. Here are a few examples of their existence which you can establish for yourself.

Sight Sensitivity

Sound Sensitivity

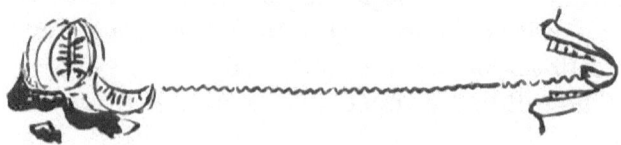

Taste Sensitivity

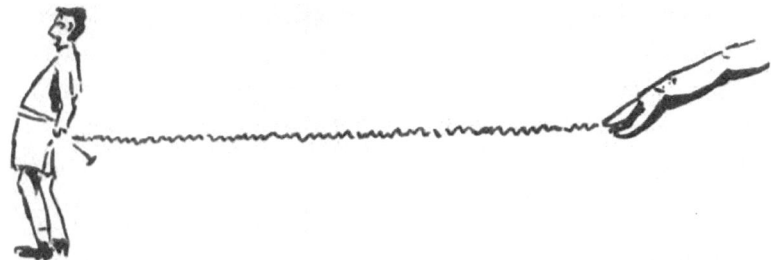

Touch Sensitivity

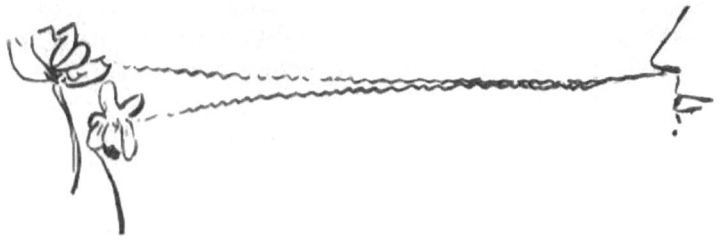

Smell Sensitivity

Temperature Sensitivity

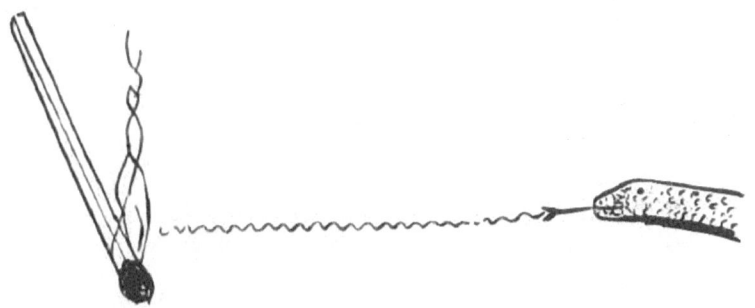

Temperature Sensitivity

Temperature sensitivity can be observed if you put a leech in a screw-top covered glass jar, and cover the sides with thick paper. If you look down into the glass jar you will see the leech standing on its tail in the centre of the jar, weaving his upper end around. Put a burning stick a foot away from one side of the jar and he will loop towards it. Move the stick to the other side and he will change direction at once.

The leech cannot smell the stick, he cannot see it, nor can he hear it, but he is so sensitive to temperature that he can feel it. Because leeches feed on the blood of animals you can understand that their 'temperature sensitivity' will lead them to sources of food.

Snakes also have a highly-developed temperature sensitivity. A snake's action of continually putting out its tongue is to guide it to warmer temperature, which to a snake may mean food (very much as if your eyes were habitually closed, but by flicking them open frequently you would be 'guided' towards light, and the light would in turn let you find food).

Vibration Sensitivity

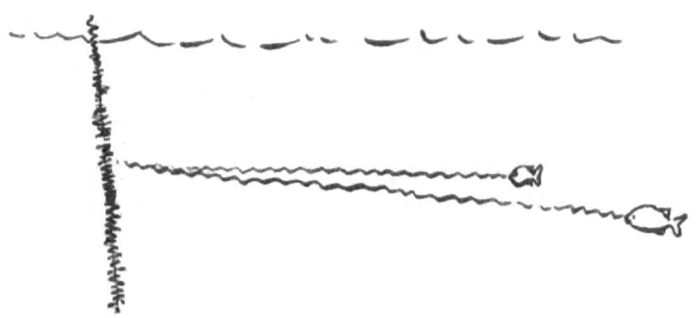

Vibration Sensitivity

Vibration sensitivity seems to be most highly developed by water living creatures. It becomes evident by the actions of fish which show themselves to be attracted to the centre of small vibrations. This can be proven by throwing fine sand into still water. Small fish will instantly dart towards the sand, but if a heavy stone is thrown, they will scatter. A thread, fastened to a stone lowered beneath the water, if pulled taut, and lightly vibrated by rubbing, will also attract small fish. Cease the rubbing, which causes the vibration in the water and the fish will disperse. Rub, and they will be attracted again.

Supersonic Sensitivity

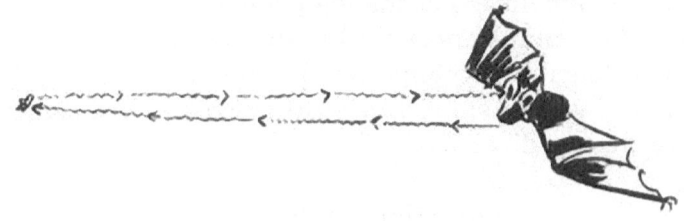

Supersonic Sensitivity

Throw a small pebble high into the air at dusk any summer evening, and watch its flight. Suddenly you will see a bat flash towards it, and then turn and fly away.

The bat sends out high pitched sound waves (beyond the pitch to which the human ear is tuned, but you may be fortunate enough to hear the 'Chirp' almost like a tightly-strung wire being plucked). These sound waves which the bat sends out in flight rebound when they meet any obstacle, even a tiny flying insect. The bat's acute ears detect and follow the 'echo' which tells it "an insect for food is over there," and so the bat turns in its flight, all the time sending out its high-pitched soundwaves, and following up the echo till it finds the insect. This is 'super-sonic sensitivity.'

No doubt the echo from the pebble becomes too strong and the flying bat sheers off to avoid a collision.

Bats, which have low power vision, can fly through a maze of crossed wires unerringly because of this supersonic sense. With fruit eating bats, or flying foxes, there appears to be an extremely acute sense of smell, and the supersonic sense does not seem to have been highly developed.

Telepathetic or "Group" Sensitivity

Group Sensitivity

This sense is seen when you watch a flight of birds, pigeons movement is not made by one bird who acts first as a leader but simultaneously by all the birds in the flight. The only feasible explanation is that they have a group sensitivity,' which, shared by all the birds in the flight, tells them to change direction.

Directional Sensitivity

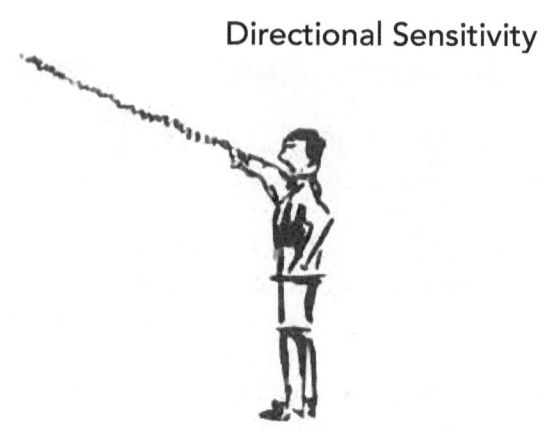

Directional Sensitivity

Directional sensitivity is fairly well spread over the animal world. Many humans have this sense, which may have been acquired by training, but whatever the explanation they show a strongly marked sense of direction. Birds show it in their ability to 'home,' and in their migratory habits. Many species of fish show it in their breeding habits, returning to spawn in the same rivers in which they themselves were hatched.

Scent Sensitivity High With Animals

Humans learn more through sight than through any other sense and as a result our sense of sight is more highly developed than any of our other senses.

As humans, we say, "There's a savage dog; look out

he doesn't see you." This is because we think all animals like ourselves depend on sight.

The savage dog will not see you at first, but he will scent you, because his nose tells him more than his eyes. This high development of 'smell sensitivity' is more common with wild creatures than their development of sight.

It is difficult for us, as humans, to think as the wild animals think. For instance, if we saw a 'snare' or trap we would be cautious. For the trap to be effective it would have to be concealed from our sight, so that we could not see it.

An animal would smell your scent on the same trap. The sight of the trap would mean nothing to it, but the man scent attached to it, and lingering possibly for weeks after it was set up, would warn the wild animal, and your trap or snare would be quite ineffective.

Until you can realise that scent (of which you are completely unaware, because you have very poor' 'smell sensitivity') tells an animal more than sight, your traps will catch nothing. This of course does not apply to all creatures. Birds and fishes are an exception, but it does apply to nearly all wild animals in their natural bush conditions.

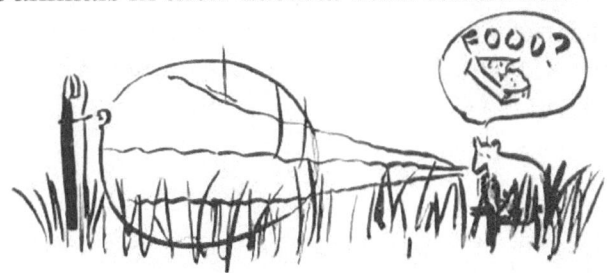

Whilst the 'man scent' may spell 'danger' under some

conditions, under other conditions where the animals have been accustomed to man and lives on his leavings (as rats, dogs and cats often do), the man scent, instead of being a warning signal, becomes a lure. Under true bush conditions, however, the 'man scent' is invariably a danger signal to all wild animals.

The man scent can be killed either by hiding it beneath a stronger smell, or by allowing it to weather off the trap or by removing it.

To 'kill' man scent you can either use a stronger scent of which the animal will not be suspicious, or you can use a scent which for one reason or another will attract the animal to your trap or snare.

This last is called a lure.

In the bush you will find many plants whose leaves when crushed have a strong perfume. If you crush these in your hands before, during, and after you have made your trap, you will leave the scent of the leaves on the trap, and this will be so much stronger than your man scent that it will drown the latter. Of course your scent will remain all round the area, and the animal will be suspicious.

Fire Removes Scent

Fire is a good destroyer of man scent, and if you scorch the trap or snare by making; a torch of dry grass or dead leaves, you will cleanse it to the animal's nose, and he will be less suspicious.

Lures

The use of a lure is undoubtedly the most effective way to kill man scent.

Urine of the species of animal you want to trap is an

excellent scent killer, and urine of a female of the species taken when she is 'on heat' or 'in season' is an infallible lure for males of that species. The urine should be taken from the bladder of a newly killed female, and bottled for future use.

Another fairly good lure is oil of aniseed, or oil of rhodiun. A very light touch of one of these lures on the bait is all that is required.

Salt is also a very effective lure in areas away from the coast, but salt is not in itself a scent killer.

Noise lures are often highly effective. These may take the form of special whistles, or may be in the form of squeaking or friction instruments. Noise lures are not commonly used in conjunction with traps or snares.

Food lures are always highly effective; small particles of food are scattered lightly around the area of the traps or snares, and the animal, scenting this food, finds it plentiful in the area, and scavenges round looking for more till finally he finds the bait in the trap, and is caught.

Obviously some of the man scent will be on the food lure particles, and, although the animal may be suspicious at first, finding that no harm comes to him, his suspicions will decrease.

An excellent use for food lure particles is to scatter them thinly along an animal trail, and then fairly thickly on either side of a simple noose snare.

Baits

In the section of this handbook dealing with animal tracks you saw that there were broadly four different divisions of animal feeding pattern. These were:

Tree feeding animals,
Earth digging and feeding animals,
Flesh eating animals,
Grazing animals.

Baits for tree feeding animals must be fruits,

Baits for earth digging animals must be roots, or insects,

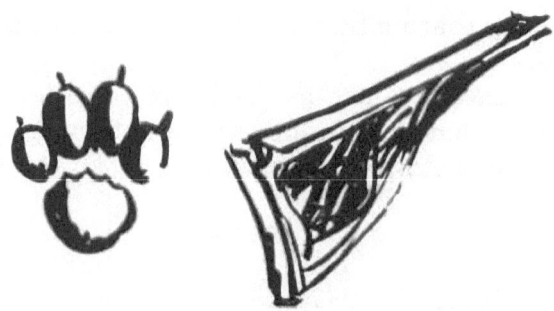

Baits for flesh eaters must be flesh,

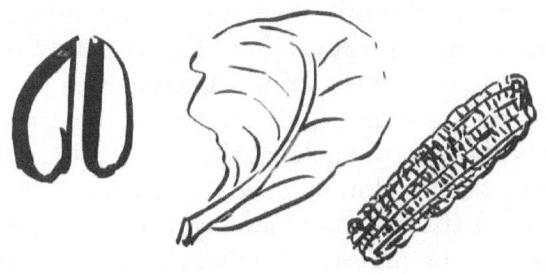

Baits for grazing animals must be herbage.

Test Baiting

Test baiting an area will show what animals are in the locality, and what baits they will take. To test bait an area select a site which is on light dusty clean soil that will clearly show all tracks. The area should be three or four yards square.

1 PUMPKIN SEED
2 CARROT
3 S. POTATO
4 BREAD
5 MAIZE
6 APPLE
7 BREAD + HONEY
8 BREAD-ANISEED
9 CABBAGE
10 S.POTATO ANISEED
11 MEAT
12 FISH HEAD
13 SORGHUM SEED A

Drive ten or a dozen short stakes, each about a foot long, into the ground. There should be at least three feet between each stake. Tie different baits, some with lures and some without to the stakes. Make a sketch map of the position of the stakes and notes of the bait each carried.

This work should be done in the afternoon. The following morning you must visit the area, and on the soft dust you will see the tracks of all the creatures which visited the area during the night, and what baits they took.

You will see bird tracks at the seeds, and tied up worm (if you put one there). You will see the tracks of tree climbing animals around the stakes where you had a piece of apple, and you will see the digging claw tracks of earth bur-rowers around a piece of sweet potato or a carrot, while a pumpkin seed will have attracted both a bush rat and a bird.

You will notice, too, that some baits, possibly those with lures, have been untouched, while others have been taken.

This work of test baiting is an essential preliminary to successful trapping. Salt is a good addition to all baits.

Suggested test baits for Australian conditions are as follows:

Roots	Flesh
Sweet potato	Meat
Carrot	Fish head
Parsnip	Worm
Dandelion root	Cheese
Yam or other ground tuber	Fruits
	Apple
Seeds and Grains	Banana
Pumpkin seed	Fig and local fruit baits
Melon seed	Herbage
Corn	Cabbage leaf
Wheat	Lettuce leaf
Sorghum seed	Celery stalk
Peanut	Carrot top
Nut	

These should be used both with and without lures.

Development of Sense Organs Indicates Degree of Sensitivity

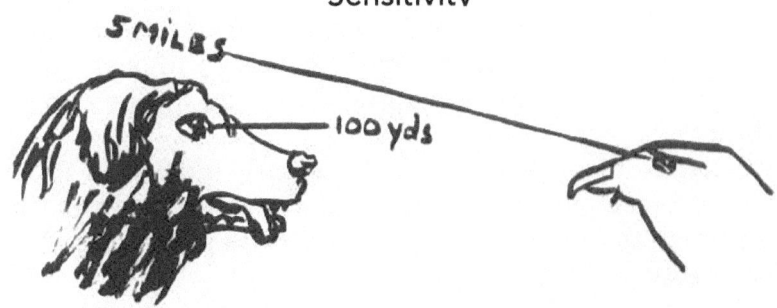

In a general way high development of sense organs indicates degree of sense dependence of the animal.

For example, animals which have large ears have acute hearing, and animals with pronounced nasal development have a sharp alertness to scent.

Sense organ development is not a mere matter of size of the organ.

A human eye, or an eagle's eye, are not as large as a dog's but the development of both the human eye and the eagle's eye far exceed the development of the dog's, they both have a far greater range of adaptability to varying conditions of light, and, something the dog's eye lacks, they are both sensitive to colour.

In the act of seeing there is first a rapid scanning of the area with the eyes. In this scanning, something, it may be movement or any departure from the normal pattern, cries 'stop' to the eyes. This is 'selection,' the second part of seeing. Having selected an object for attention, the third stage, 'recognition,' commences, and only when this is completed do we 'perceive' or 'see.

The eye does this continually, and is adapted for 'seeing' under a wide range of light conditions. It also has the ability to see colour and can discern and perceive over a wide range of distances.

In contrast to the human eye with its high state of development, compare the human nose. Its development is so poor that it is of little use

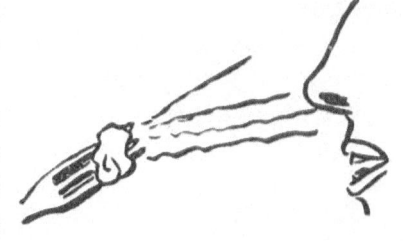

19

as an aid to living. If the meat on your fork is bad your nose might possibly detect the odour, or if cloth is burning you might smell it, but when you consider the scent sensitivity of a deer or a dog which can smell you half a mile downwind, it is apparent that the human nose tells its owner literally nothing.

Since size alone is not a definite indication of the extent of development of a sense organ, you must rely on your observation to tell you which of an animal's sense organs are most highly developed.

For instance, a dog's nose does not appear to be extremely well developed physically. It is not unduly large, as is the nose of an elephant (its trunk), or the nose and nostrils of a deer, horse or cow.

But by observation, that is 'seeing' and deduction you will learn that a dog's nose is its most highly developed organ, and therefore its most important sense for 'living,' with 'hearing' as the next sense, and 'sight' last on the list.

Watch a dog looking for a stone which you have thrown. His eyes follow it in flight, but when he is seeking where he thinks it has fallen you see him running round with his nose to the ground, and it is his nose, and not his eyes which find the stone for him, and he selects the stone from among hundreds of others solely because it has your scent on it.

Watch a horse when you hold a carrot out to him on the palm of your hand. First he puts his nostrils to if, rarely if ever his eyes, then he takes it in his lips.

When a Sense organ is Highly Developed the Animal Makes Use of that Sense Organ in Preference to its Other Senses

In a general way an animal's feeding habits tell you much about its sense development. For instance all digging animals must have a strong scent development in order to find food hidden in the earth.

All flesh eating animals must have good near sight development to stalk and find their food. They must also have a good distant scent development to be aware of food which may be hidden and out of direct sight.

All grazing animals must have very good scent development to select the choice morsels of herbage for their food, and also to warn them of an approaching enemy. They also must have good hearing development, and finally they must have good sight development to recognise an enemy and to see which is the best direction for escape. Since many grazing animals feed by night as well as by day,; the eye must be very large in size in order to take in more light at night, but this is purely a matter of size and not necessarily of actual development or high sensitivity.

Similarity of Form Does Not Mean Similarity of Habit

Animals which appear similar in shape and form do not necessarily have similar habits. Rabbits and hares are similar in shape and form and feeding habits, but very different in habits.

Rabbits, as you know, live in colonies underground, but hares live singly in a 'form,' or nest, on the surface.

When a rabbit is alarmed it seeks safety in the warren.

When a hare is alarmed it seeks its safety in running at speed. A rabbit is attracted by newly dug earth. A hare prefers grassland and avoids new ground.

This dissimilarity of animal habits within their own family group or species exists throughout the whole animal kingdom.

One type of wild dog will hunt in packs, and another will hunt singly, as does the fox. One member of the cat family will climb trees, and pounce on its prey from overhead: another species will stalk its prey at a drinking pool and make its kill there.

One species of kangaroo or deer will live on open plains, and another species will avoid open country, and live only in forest land, while yet another species prefers hilly or rocky country. One type of pigeon feeds solely on fruits growing on trees and another type will prefer ground feeding, selecting fruits which have fallen to the ground, and ground growing seeds and grain.

The Balance of Nature

Over countless ages a balance between the different forms of life has been attained.

As a simple example, if all the animals of a country were grass eating, there would be no check on their population growth, the grass which is their food would eventually be destroyed, and as a species the grass eating animals would die out in a couple of generations. There would be no balance.

Introduce flesh-eating animals into these conditions. They live on the grass eaters, and also on one another, and the population of all is kept at a lower level. Further, the weaker animals are killed off, and the stronger alone survive to breed. In a short time a balance between grass eaters and flesh eaters has been achieved.

This is the balance of nature.

Continuous destruction of wild life can easily upset this balance, and, like a chain reaction, the unbalance spreads. The uneven balance of nature can also be caused by the introduction of either a plant or animal foreign to the country.

In one part of New Zealand domestic cats gone wild

became a plague. The cat plague was finally traced to the introduction of red clover.

It happened this way. The red clover is very deep throated, and only one species of bee could extract the nectar. This species of bee made its hive in the earth. With the plentiful supply of honey, this type of bee increased rapidly. A certain type of field mice liked the honey of this bee, and they too increased in population, feeding on the earth hives of the red clover bees. With the increase of mouse population the cat population flourished until finally the cats assumed plague proportions.

Excessive trapping also can upset this balance of nature, but trapping used intelligently can help nature to restore its balance. Trapping can also be extremely valuable as an aid to the extermination of pests.

Trapping and Character Training

It has been shown that TRAPPING calls not only for an extensive knowledge of the mechanics of bush-made traps, but also for a thorough study of the habits and ways of life of all wild creatures.

The person who undertakes the work of trapping, whether for a livelihood or as a means of studying wild creatures at close quarters (as the artist and the zoologist must do) must be a person of wide understanding and great tolerance.

Trapping naturally brings about a love of wild animals, because it effects a full and complete understanding of their ways of life.

No true trapper could be cruel to wild creatures. His sympathies are too large to endure cruelty. The best way in the world to engender a love of wild animals is to be a trapper. Only then can you realise how intelligent and lovable all the wild creatures are.

This does not apply to the average professional rabbit-trapper, who is a trapper solely because it provides him with an easy means of making money quickly.

There are exceptions, too, among wild dog hunters, or 'doggers.' Many doggers relish the challenge which is put up to them by a savagely intelligent 'killer' dog with a big reward on its scalp. For these, the dogger has to use all his skill and cunning to match that of the wild dog.

To be efficient in trapping work the trapper must possess infinite patience, he must be able to stalk a wild animal in order to observe it at close quarters. He must learn about its sensitivities. In this and all the other work called for in trapping his own sensitivities are sharpened, and his intelligence and observation developed to a remarkable degree.

No people equal the native in powers of observation and deduction. This is due to the single fact that the native depends solely upon his hunting for his food.

What hunting has done for the native in perfection of his powers of observation, trapping can do for the white man to a lesser degree.

This development of observation and cultivation of the powers of deduction, coupled to the painstaking care which is necessary to all trapping work, play a major part of character development of an individual.

For example, in stalking an animal to observe it at reasonably close quarters, the would-be trapper soon learns that he must approach up wind, he learns to take advantage of every scrap of cover, and to avoid showing himself on the skyline. He learns that he can approach the animal more easily if he keeps still when the wind is still, and moves when gusts of wind move the bushes, stirring them into action. Only then will his movements pass unseen by the animal he is stalking. With the development of his observation, and aided by his intelligence he soon finds out that he can place an obvious object such as a piece of white rag on a distant bush where it will constantly attract the animal's suspicious attention, and, taking advantage of this, he can circle and approach from the opposite direction.

The making of a trap out of bush materials calls for a ready eye to see the right sticks quickly, and requires cunning, and co-ordination of head and hand to cut and shape the sticks correctly. Having made the trap, it must be sited in the right place, and then watched. All this calls for observation and infinite patience. Once the animal is caught there comes with its capture an appreciation of its apparent helplessness, and a sympathy with its predicament. This in turn leads to a genuine love of all wild life.

Is Trapping Cruel?

Nature lovers will contend that trapping is cruel and unnecessary.

Undoubtedly this is true of much of the trapping which takes place now, and has taken place in the past. Trapping for the skins is cruel, wasteful and not in any way productive of good. Similarly in other countries trapping of animals for the pelts threatened whole species of wildlife with extinction.

The general run of mechanical trapping is extremely cruel. Most animal traps are similar to the common rabbit trap. A device with two steel jaws that clamp onto an animal's leg generally breaks it, and holds the creature in agony until it is killed, possibly hours later, by the trapper.

These traps are not discriminatory. Protected animals and even birds are caught in rabbit traps set near warrens by river banks. Pets, too, are caught and their legs broken so they either have to be destroyed or left maimed for life. Trapping of this nature is cruel and wasteful.

Trapping can be humane, and need not in any way cause suffering or extreme distress to the wild animal. Pen and box type traps can be used to catch animals alive. These type of traps cause the animals no discomfort or pain. Other types of traps such as logfalls kill instantly. The wild creature is not left in lingering agony for hours. When it touches the bait, death is merciful, and instant.

It is vitally important in all trapping work that you should never leave the trap, if set, unattended for more than a few hours.

A set but unattended trap may catch and hold an animal captive. The animal in the trap may either perish through lack of water or food, or may dig its way out, if the pen of the trap is made of stakes driven into the ground.

The trapping of small birds such as painted finches, larks, thrushes, lovebirds and parrots, where it is desired to capture them for sale into captivity, is cruel. It may be argued that these creatures' lives are more secure when caged, and have freedom equal to their wild life if under proper conditions.

The trouble is that they rarely are under proper natural conditions when in captivity, and except for the 'lure' type of cage trap, the trapping methods are cruel, and very destructive of life. (The method of trapping small birds for pets usually makes use of snares on a stick set in a bush or tree which the birds frequent.)

This writer recommends to every bush-lover that if they ever see a snare stick they should destroy it immediately, without any regard for the feelings of the person who made it and placed it.

It will be argued also by many bush-lovers that it is not in the best interest of the community to make information about trapping or traps public. These people will delude themselves into the belief that small boys will set up traps and snares indiscriminately, to the immediate peril and destruction of all wild life. They will argue too that all trapping is cruel, and unnecessary. No bush-bred boy will trap unnecessarily, and no city-bred boy would have the essential knowledge of the wild to be able to trap anything with effect. Trapping is not effective unless the trapper completely understands the habits and life of the wild creatures. This is something completely foreign to the city-bred boy.

Reasons for Trapping

The trapping of wild creatures, whether bird or animal, can only be justified on the grounds of 'Preservation.' Some wild animals prey on other less-aggressive species—particularly is this true of the domestic cat, which, having gone bush, becomes the No. 1 killer of wild life. Cats are difficult to poison. They regurgitate the bait and continue their destruction unaffected. Fortunately they are comparatively easy to trap and when captured can be destroyed. Dogs which have gone bush, or which have mated with wild dogs, and also foxes, rank with cats as destroyers of native life.